19, 95

THE HISPANIC INFLUENCE IN THE UNITED STATES

LATINOS

IN AMERICAN HISTORY

CESAR CHAVEZ

BY KATHLEEN TRACY

Mitchell Lane
PUBLISHERS

P.O. Box 196
Hockessin, Delaware 19707

THE HISPANIC INFLUENCE IN THE UNITED STATES

LATINOS
IN AMERICAN HISTORY

OTHER TITLES IN THE SERIES

Visit us on the web: www.mitchelllane.com
Comments? email us: mitchelllane@mitchelllane.com

THE HISPANIC INFLUENCE IN THE UNITED STATES

LATINOS
IN AMERICAN HISTORY

CESAR
CHAVEZ

BY KATHLEEN TRACY

Printing 1   2   3   4   5   6   7   8   9

Library of Congress Cataloging-in-Publication Data

Tracy, Kathleen.
    Cesar Chavez / by Kathleen Tracy.
            p. cm. — (Latinos in American history)
Includes bibliographical references and index.
    ISBN 1-58415-224-9 (Library Bound)
    1. Chavez, Cesar, 1927- 2. Labor leaders—United States—Biography. 3. Mexican Americans—Biography. 4. Agricultural laborers—Labor unions—United States—History—20th century. I. Title. II. Series.
    HD6509.C48T73 2003
    331.88'13'092--dc21
                                                                            2003004651

ABOUT THE AUTHOR: Kathleen Tracy has been a journalist for over twenty years. Her writing has been featured in magazines including The Toronto Star's "Star Week," *A&E Biography* magazine, *KidScreen* and *TV Times*. She is also the author of numerous biographies including "The Boy Who Would Be King" (Dutton), "Jerry Seinfeld - The Entire Domain" (Carol Publishing), "Don Imus - America's Cowboy" (Carroll & Graf), "Mariano Guadalupe Vallejo," and "William Hewlett: Pioneer of the Computer Age," both for Mitchell Lane. She recently completed "God's Will?" for Sourcebooks.

PHOTO CREDITS: Cover: AP Photo; p. 8 Corbis; p. 10 Hulton/Archive; p. 12 Walter P. Reuther Library, Wayne State University; p. 18 Walter P. Reuther Library, Wayne State University; p. 22 Hulton/Archive; p. 24 Walter P. Reuther Library, Wayne State University; p. 27 AP Photo; p. 28 Hulton/Archive; p. 30 AP Photo; p. 36 Corbis

PUBLISHER'S NOTE: This story is based on the author's extensive research, which she believes to be accurate. Documentation of this research can be found on page 45.

    The spelling of the names in this book follow the generally accepted usage of modern day. The spelling of Spanish names in English has evolved over time with no consistency. Many names have been anglicized and no longer use the accent marks or any Spanish grammar. Others have retained the Spanish grammar. Hence, we refer to Hernando De Soto as "De Soto," but Francisco Vásquez de Coronado as "Coronado." There are other variances as well. Some sources might spell Vásquez as Vazquez. For the most part, we have adapted the more widely recognized spellings.

CONTENTS

Since the United States is home to many natural resources, they are often taken for granted. The drought that turned Oklahoma into a "Dust Bowl" during the 1930s taught us the importance of maintaining our natural resources.

DARK DAYS

America has always been seen as the land of plenty. There are mighty rivers and lakes to supply our water, coal and oil reserves to give us power, and vast areas of fertile farmland capable of feeding us all. However, it's important to take care of our natural resources because the results can be disastrous if we don't. Never was this lesson more painfully learned than in the 1930s.

After the end of World War I, a recession caused the prices paid for farm crops to decrease. To continue making the same amount of money, farmers in the southern Great Plains, the vast flat area in the middle of the country that includes Oklahoma, Kansas and Nebraska, increased production so they had more crops to sell. To do this, they cultivated more land.

But this land they were using wasn't intended to be farmland. It was grassland that had been used as pasture for livestock. Because soil conservation was not widely practiced at that time, the result was fields with shallow topsoil that was less able to hold moisture. When a severe seven-year drought that began in 1931 hit the Great Plains, the soil began to erode. A series of dust

A severe drought in the 1930s during the Great Depression turned once-thriving farms into patches of dust. Unable to grow crops or make a living, farmers abandoned their homes, like the one pictured here, and traveled to California looking for work as farm laborers.

storms hit the region in 1932. Many farms literally dried up and blew away in the wind. About 150,000 square miles of land in the Southern Great Plains came to be called the Dust Bowl.

Making matters even worse, the country was in the midst of the Great Depression, which began after the stock market crashed in 1929. During the worst days of the Depression, one out of every four Americans was unemployed and desperate to find work. Many farmers had taken out loans in order to pay for machines to help them cultivate greater areas of land when the recession first hit. Banks demanded that these loans be repaid. Many farmers didn't have the money. So they lost their land and their homes.

Now homeless and out of work, thousands of farmers and their families packed their few belongings in their cars. They headed west to California, which even then was a world leader in agriculture. The flood of unemployed from the southern Great Plains that swarmed to California became known as "Okies." Many were from Oklahoma, the state hardest hit by the drought.

With its rich central valley and warm climate, California was able to grow a wide variety of produce. Its growing season lasted year round, meaning there was always the need for migrant farm workers to pick and harvest the crops. But the pay was low and the living conditions terrible. When working the fields, most migrant workers lived in dingy overcrowded quarters that lacked bathrooms, electricity, or running water. Some even had to live in their cars. Author John Steinbeck wrote a Pulitzer Prize-winning novel called *Grapes of Wrath* that vividly depicts the hardships these families endured.

To the Okies' bitter disappointment, California didn't prove to be the promised land they had hoped for. For one thing, the Depression had hit many California farmers just as hard. Many of them were forced to scrounge for work. Also, California already had a large pool of migrant workers—Mexican immigrants as well as Mexican-American farm hands who had been working the land for over 50 years.

Many new arrivals didn't know the deep ties these workers had to the land. California had been claimed by Spain early in the sixteenth century. When Mexico became independent from Spain in 1821, California became part of the new nation.

However, following the Mexican War of 1846-1848, the United States acquired a huge area of land that included California, Texas, Arizona, and New Mexico, as well as large parts of Colorado, Nevada and Utah. At the time, approximately 80,000 to 100,000 Mexicans were living in the region. Under the terms of the 1848 Treaty of Guadalupe Hidalgo, they were made U.S. citizens. Even so, as settlers from the east settled in the newly conquered territory, these Mexican Americans were considered second-class citizens. Frequently they could only find the lowest,

Cesar met many migrant families while living in workers' camps. Here, a migrant mother is shown with three of her seven children at a farm workers' camp.

least appealing jobs. Shockingly, in Texas, some were actually put into slavery up until the Civil War.

During the Mexican Revolution, which lasted from 1910 to 1917, many Mexicans traveled across the border into California and other southwestern states. They found work on the railroads, in mines and as migrant farm hands. Despite being in the country illegally, the United States government didn't care. The outbreak of World War I caused severe labor shortages. In fact, some unions, organizations whose purpose is to protect workers' rights, actively encouraged Mexican workers to become members.

In 1928, the Confederacion de Uniones Obreras Mexicanas (CUOM) was specifically formed to organize Mexican workers in the U.S. These unions were considered militant because of their aggressive pursuit of fair wages and better working conditions. As the unions became more powerful, organizers were able to call for strikes in order to force companies to pay fair salaries.

However, as the Great Depression raged and more and more Okies poured into California looking for work, the attitude toward Mexican laborers in general underwent a dramatic change. Prejudice against Mexican nationals grew. It was especially strong among desperate unemployed "Anglos," a term often used for those who spoke English. They resented "foreign" workers taking away jobs, however menial they might be.

This intolerance led to mass deportations of Mexicans who had lived and worked in the United States for years. U.S.-born Mexican Americans, many of whom had also lost farms during the Depression, were also the target of prejudice. Even though they worked side by side in the fields during the day, Anglos and Mexican Americans stayed in segregated camps at night. This anti-Mexican sentiment and the loss of so many members weakened the strength of the unions. As a result of this setback, working conditions deteriorated.

It was in this environment that a young boy named Cesar Chavez grew up. Instead of being overwhelmed or made bitter by the inhumane conditions around him, Cesar's experiences turned him into a nonviolent activist for change. In the end, he would almost single-handedly change the way farm workers are treated and seen in the United States.■

Cesar's family and friends celebrate his father's 100th birthday. Standing (L to R): Cesar, Ricardo Chavez, Vickey Lastra, Fr. Luis Baldomado, Rita Medina, and Librado Chavez, Jr. Sitting: Librado and Juana Chavez.

THE DEPRESSION HITS HOME

Sometime during the 1880s a young man named Cesario Chavez was among a steady stream of Mexican immigrants who traveled across the border looking for a better way of life. He had been born as a peon, or farm worker, in Chihuahua, Mexico. Cesario and his wife, Dorotea, settled near Yuma, Arizona. They established themselves as farmers, homesteading more than one hundred acres in the Gila Valley and raising a large family of 15 children. The family home was built to last. It had adobe walls that were more than 18 inches thick. Those walls kept the family cool in the summer and warm on cold winter nights.

Though most of the children moved on, son Librado followed in his parents' footsteps. He and his wife, Juana Estrada, who had also come from Chihuahua, worked very hard and became somewhat prominent members of the Yuma community. In addition to farming the family ranch, Librado was elected to be the local postmaster and ran a general store. A service station and pool hall were attached to it.

On March 31, 1927, the second of their five children was born. As the first son, his parents named him Cesar, after his grandfather. Librado was a loving father but he worked long hours and wasn't able to spend as much time with his children as he would have liked. That meant that Cesar and his siblings spent a lot of time with their mother.

The family lived in an apartment above the store. Although there was never much money and their surroundings were modest, much of Cesar's childhood was happy.

One reason was that he was part of a big family. Cesar grew up surrounded by many aunts and uncles as well as siblings. His two closest friends as a youngster were his cousin Manuel and his brother Richard, and the three were inseparable. They enjoyed playing outside, swimming in irrigation canals and playing pool at their father's business.

Cesar was also close to his older sister, Rita. Because Juana was often busy helping Librado in the fields or at one of their businesses, Rita helped to raise her younger brothers.

Even as a youngster, Cesar was stubborn—a quality that would help him in his later life. Rita remembered how that stubbornness showed itself when she took him to school for the first time.

According to *The Fight in the Fields*, "The six-year-old flatly refused to sit anywhere except with his beloved sister. He warned the teacher that if he couldn't sit with his sister, he was going home. Sure enough, once Rita managed to extricate (remove) herself from the arms of a tearful, clinging Cesar, he fled out the door and raced down the road. After Rita caught up to him and coaxed him back, the teacher asked two second graders to pull up an extra desk near his sister. 'So Cesar sat by me,' Rita laughs. 'After two or three days—I can't remember how many— he finally agreed to go with the first graders, but he won that first battle there and then.'"

What Juana lacked in material possessions, she made up for in warmth and spiritual faith, creating a loving home for her family. Juana was devoutly religious and taught her children that more could be accomplished through peace than through violence.

As a youngster, Cesar almost always lived up to her teachings. Usually he walked away from fights at school. Once, however, one of his older cousins threatened to throw Cesar's cat into a ditch filled with water. Cesar grabbed a shotgun and the cousin ran away. But the gun wasn't loaded.

She also instilled in her children the importance of helping others who were less fortunate than themselves. During the early years of the Depression, unemployed men would pass through the Yuma area looking for work. Although Juana and Librado had no jobs to offer, they would frequently invite these strangers into their home for dinner. They also extended credit to customers who were experiencing hard times. Such examples of compassion and caring would make a lasting impression on young Cesar.

Eventually, the Chavez family began to feel the effects of the Depression. Because many of the customers to whom they'd given credit couldn't pay their bills, they finally had to sell their businesses. The family moved back to the ranch.

At first things were all right. They could grow food and raise chickens. There were eggs and milk for the growing children, and even some left over to sell.

But the drought struck the Southwest as well. That made raising crops difficult and by 1936 Librado was struggling to pay even the most basic of bills. Suddenly, the prospect of losing the family home loomed as a very real possibility.

Years earlier, Cesar's father had agreed to clear 80 acres of land in exchange for the deed to 40 acres of land that adjoined the family home. But the neighbor reneged on the deal and sold the land to another man. Librado consulted with a lawyer, who advised him his best option was to take out a loan and buy the land rather than to try and enforce the original agreement.

Now there was no money to make the loan payments or the taxes on the property. In 1938, it was put up for public auction and the Chavez family had to leave. That would change their lives forever. It was also an injustice that the 11-year-old would never forget.

Librado, Juana and their five children packed as many belongings as they could fit into their 10-year-old car. They headed for California in search of farm work, since it was the one skill they knew best. They joined an estimated 300,000 other migrant workers who scratched out a living by "following the crops," traveling all over the state to pick whatever was in season. But they were ill-prepared for the hardships and the prejudice that lay ahead.

"Those early days when we first came to California were rough," Cesar recalled in the book, *Huelga! The First Hundred Days of the Great Delano Grape Strike* by Eugene Nelson. "We were really green, and whenever a labor contractor told us something, we fell for it hook, line and sinker."

After the family arrived in California, a labor contractor signed Librado to harvest wine grapes near Fresno.

"They were bad grapes; there were very few bunches on the vines, and we were the only family working in the field. But we were too green to wonder why we were the only ones," Chavez told Nelson.

After picking grapes for an entire week, Librado asked that they be paid. The contractor informed them that workers normally didn't get their money until the contractor was paid by the winery. But after Librado convinced the contractor they literally had no food and were starving, the contractor "loaned" him 20 dollars and assured them they'd be getting a big check once the winery paid. The family survived on the 20 dollars for the next seven weeks as they continued to work the fields. When they were finally finished, the family went to the contractor's house.

It was empty. The man had skipped out, taking all their hard-earned money with him.

Cesar and his family were in a desperate situation. When another contractor told them there was good money to be made picking cotton near the town of Mendota, west of Fresno, they headed there. By this time it was November and the rainy season had started. There was hardly any work. To survive, they fished and cut wild mustard greens and lived in a migrant camp. When everyone else moved on to find other work, the Chavezes found themselves stranded. They had no money to even buy gas.

As he explained to Nelson, "When everyone else left they shut off the lights, so we sat around in the dark. We finally got a few dollars from some relatives in Arizona and bought enough gas for our old Studebaker to get us to Los Angeles. Our car broke down in L.A. (Los Angeles) and my mother sold crocheting on the street to raise the money for enough gas to get to Brawley (a small town in the Imperial Valley, about 100 miles east of San Diego). We lived for three days in our car in Brawley before we could find a house we could afford to rent."

Their first experience as migrant workers had left them all numb. Cesar had been exposed to unimaginable poverty and physical hardship, enduring scorching heat in the summer and bone-chilling cold rain in the winter. But even more emotionally devastating would be the unexpected prejudice he would experience in California as an American of Mexican descent.■

César poses for his 8th grade graduation picture. He and other children of migrant workers were often ridiculed at school for speaking Spanish and for having to live in run-down camps. His family was so poor Cesar would make extra money by collecting silver cigarette wrappers from the highways.

CHAPTER
3

CHILD OF THE FIELDS

Although Brawley would become their home base, there wasn't enough work to support them all year. Every spring, Cesar and his family would hit the road, traveling through central California. They'd pick peas, lettuce, tomatoes, figs, prunes, grapes and apricots. Then in late November, they would go back south, praying their old car wouldn't break down before they made it back to Brawley.

As they adjusted to the migrant way of life, Cesar's family learned how to better survive. When they couldn't find housing, or couldn't afford it, they camped under bridges. They quickly learned the order the various crops came to harvest so they could find work at peak pay. In keeping with their belief in helping others, Librado and Juana shared the lessons they had so painfully learned with others to keep them from making the same mistakes they had at first.

Despite their transient lifestyle, Cesar continued to go to school whenever he could. He would later estimate he had attended over 30 different schools. Although he was naturally bright and inquisitive, he struggled because his family only spoke Spanish at home. Most of his teachers were Anglo and only spoke English. In fact, Spanish was forbidden in school, even on the playground. Cesar's punishment for speaking his native language was being rapped across his knuckles with a ruler. It was very painful.

He often found his teachers to be distant and almost disinterested. Because migrant children tended to move on after a short while, it seemed as if it wasn't worth the effort to get too involved with them.

But what bothered Cesar the most was that Mexicans and Anglos were kept separated from each other in the schools. "There was a school and there was an annex," he is quoted in *Huelga! The First Hundred Days of the Great Delano Grape Strike.* "The Mexican-American kids went to the annex—it was just another name for the segregated school."

Although Cesar liked learning, he didn't like the conflicts he saw between Mexican Americans and Anglos. In Arizona, the Mexican-American farmers and Anglo farmers had been equals. But there was a different sentiment in California. In Brawley the Mexican Americans all lived in one section of town. They were expected to understand they were not welcome in the Anglo section.

But Cesar and his brother Richard were used to going wherever they wanted. They were oblivious to the prejudice directed at them until a traumatic incident opened their eyes. Looking to make some extra money, Cesar and Richard put together a shoeshine kit and sought out customers on the street. They earned enough money to buy lunch so they headed for a restaurant that sold the best hamburgers in the valley. They paid no attention to the sign in the window that read *WHITES ONLY* and ran in to order two hamburgers.

According to Nelson, the waitress refused to serve them and ordered the boys out of the restaurant. She said, "What's matter, you dumb Mex—can't you read?" as she pointed to the sign. Richard was enraged but Cesar was completely humiliated. He had been born in America, as had his father. Yet he was being treated as if he were some kind of outsider who wasn't good enough to patronize the same places Anglos did.

Life seemed to become a series of humiliations. During the winter of 1939, Cesar and his family became stranded in Oxnard, a city along the Southern California coast, when their car broke down and they ended up spending the winter in a tent.

"We were the only people there living in a tent and everyone ridiculed us," Cesar admitted. (Nelson, *Huelga!*) "We went to bed at dusk because there was no light. My mother and father got up at 5:30 in the morning to go pick peas. It cost $70 to go to the fields and back, and some days they did not even make enough for their transportation."

To help out, Cesar and Richard began walking along the side of the highway, looking for empty cigarette packages. They weren't interested in finding cigarettes. They wanted the small pieces of tinfoil that lined the packages. They eventually collected enough to make a huge ball out of the foil. It weighed 18 pounds. The previous winter Cesar had been forced to walk to school barefoot because the family had been too poor to buy him shoes. So he and his brother sold their foil to a Mexican junk dealer. He paid them enough to buy a pair of tennis shoes and two sweatshirts.

Cesar was 12 years old when John Steinbeck's *The Grapes of Wrath* was published in 1939. The book caused a sensation because it put a spotlight on the plight of migrant workers for the first time. However, the increased enlightenment of the American public did little to improve the migrant workers' lot. If anything, landowners and labor contractors dug their heels in even more aggressively against any attempts to unionize the workers. That didn't stop the workers from fighting back.

"About 1939 we were living in San Jose. One of the old CIO unions began organizing workers in the dried fruit industry," Cesar said, according to author Nelson. Although Librado had never been an active participant in any union, this time he took out a union card.

"Sometimes the men would meet at our house and I remember seeing their picket signs and hearing them talk," Cesar told Nelson. "They had a strike and my father and uncle picketed at night. It made a deep impression on me. But of course they lost the strike and that was the end of the union. But from that time on my father joined every new agricultural union that came along—often he was the first one to join."

Despite moving around so much, Cesar was still able to graduate from grade school in 1942 as an eighth grader, a significant achievement among children of migrant workers. But it would be the end of his formal education.

After the attack on Pearl Harbor brought the US into World War II, Cesar joined the Army.

While Cesar would have liked the chance to go on to high school, Librado had suffered an injury that prevented him from working. Cesar couldn't stand the idea of his mother going back to work in the fields. So he quit school and became a full-time migrant farm worker. In whatever spare time he had, Cesar would read avidly, intent on educating himself.

In December 1941, the Japanese attacked Pearl Harbor and America entered World War II. Many American farm workers entered the armed forces. As a result, there was suddenly a short-age of laborers to work the fields so in the summer of 1942, the *bracero* program was instituted. Under the terms of the agree-ment, U.S. officials would give temporary jobs to Mexican farm laborers in U.S. farm fields. When the contracts expired, the *braceros* were required to turn in their permits and return to Mexico.

Mexican workers poured across the border because they saw the United States as the land of opportunity. Farmers took ad-vantage of this law by primarily hiring *braceros*. They realized that *braceros* would work longer days for less pay and would tolerate the often horrendous working conditions.

In addition, using the *braceros* undermined union organizing efforts. Employers were now forcing all workers to sign what were called "yellow-dog contracts," in which they promised not to join a union while employed. As Cesar traveled around on his own, following the crops, he got to know many Anglo workers and realized that they endured the same problems the Mexican-American workers suffered and longed to do something about it. But people were afraid to speak out, fearful of losing their jobs, no matter how meager the work. Cesar promised himself that one day, he would find a way to make conditions better for all of them.■

Cesar and his wife Helen worked together to improve the lives of migrant workers.

CHAPTER 4

AN INCREASING AWARENESS

With the war still raging, Cesar joined the Navy in 1944 at the age of 17.

According to the book *The Fight in the Fields*, he said, "I was doing sugar-beet thinning, the worst backbreaking job, and I remember telling my father, 'Dad, I've had it!' Neither my mother nor father wanted me to go, but I joined up anyway."

Cesar spent his tour of duty on a variety of ships and shore assignments in the Pacific Ocean. Although he was proud to serve his country, he was appalled at the discrimination he witnessed against Mexican Americans in the military. He never reacted with anger; instead it simply furthered his resolve to work towards ending prejudice—somehow, someway.

The Navy wasn't the only place where he found discrimination. During a three-day leave (time away from his duties) he decided to go to a movie in Delano, a small town north of Bakersfield. Like many other places in town, the theater was segregated with a designated "Whites Only" section. This time, Cesar decided to take a stand. Here he was, serving in the military, potentially risking his life for his country that proclaimed all men were created equal. Yet someone was trying to say where he could sit to watch a movie that cost him the same as it cost the Anglos.

Cesar sat down in the "Whites Only" section and waited. It was only a moment before an usher rushed up, tapped him on the arm and told him he'd have to move to the other side of the aisle. When Cesar politely refused, the manager called the police. Cesar was arrested and taken to the local police station. He was never prosecuted, but the incident marked the beginning of his social activism.

After completing his Navy enlistment and receiving an honorable discharge, Cesar returned to California. His family had rented a small cottage in the East San Jose barrio of *Sal Si Puedes*, which roughly translates to "get out if you can." As typically happens, the war had a positive effect on the economy and there were many new jobs available in West Coast shipyards and defense plants. However, while many of the Okie farm workers were able to take advantage of these opportunities and leave their migrant lifestyles behind, few Mexican-American migrants were able to move up. So Cesar once again took to the road in search of work.

One of the towns where Cesar found work was Delano. Just before entering the Navy, he had become friends with a girl his age named Helen Fabela. She worked as a clerk in a grocery store patronized by the migrant workers. Although he often had no money, Helen didn't seem to mind. She happily treated Cesar to a movie and enjoyed going for long walks with him.

The couple was married in 1948. For their honeymoon, they traveled up and down the California coast visiting all the missions from Sonoma to San Diego. They settled in Delano, living in a one-room shack, and in a short time started their family. In all, they would eventually raise eight children. Helen shared her husband's passion for social justice and compassion towards

Cesar's wife and children at the family home in La Paz, California on July 24, 2000. From left: Paul, Eloise, Anna, Sylvia, Liz, Helen, Linda and Anthony.

people. Together they began to teach the illiterate Mexican farm workers to read and write.

Cesar also continued to work the fields. He preferred working in the vineyards because grape pickers generally stayed in the same place for a longer time. But wherever he went, he saw labor contractors and land owners exploiting the workers. He tried to convince the farm owners to increase the pay and improve the working conditions but he was ignored.

Cesar would later recount a turning point in his young life to writer Wendy Goepel for a 1964 *Farm Labor* interview.

"When I was 19," he recalled, "I was picking cotton in Corcoran. A car with loud speakers came around. The speakers were saying: '*Stop Working. You're not making a living. Come down-*

town to a rally instead.' My brother and I left, with many others. Seven thousand cotton pickers gathered in a little park in the center of Corcoran. There was a platform and a union leader got up and started talking to all the workers about 'the cause.' I would have died right then if someone had told me how and why to die for our cause. But no one did. There was a crisis, and a mob and nothing came of it all. A week later everyone was back picking cotton in the same field at the same low wages. It was dramatic. People came together. Then it was over."

The experience was an epiphany for Cesar. He realized that there was no organization to help support farm workers. Without an organization, there was little hope.

Chavez was inspired by Gandhi's philosophy of change through non-violence.

Cesar continued working but now he looked for any opportunity to get more involved. Soon afterward he joined the National Agricultural Workers Union. But it was no more successful than any other union that tried to organize farm workers.

In 1948, he participated in his first strike, protesting low wages and poor working conditions. However, after only a few days the strike was broken and the workers were forced back to the fields. Cesar knew real change would only come with perseverance and patience.

Back in San Jose, Cesar met Father Donald McDonnell, a Catholic priest from San Francisco sent to work with the farm laborers and *braceros*. Father McDonnell taught the workers about the Church's social doctrines on labor organizing and social justice, which had a tremendous influence and impact on Cesar. He would also talk to Father McDonnell one-on-one for hours.

As a result, Cesar began a serious, in-depth study of papal encyclicals on labor, books on labor history and the teachings of St. Francis of Assisi. His reading also included Louis Fisher's *The Life of Gandhi*, which promoted the principles and philosophy of nonviolence. Mahatma Gandhi helped free the Indian people from British rule through nonviolent resistance, and is honored by his people as the father of the nation of India.

Cesar's increasing activism eventually brought him to the attention of other well-known organizers. The government-run farm labor camp that Steinbeck depicted in *The Grapes of Wrath* was based on the Sunset Camp, located south of Bakersfield. The man who ran the camp was Fred Ross, an influential community organizer whose career spanned seven decades.

In 1952, Ross was organizing the Community Service Organization (CSO), one of the most effective civil rights groups among Latinos in California. Ross sought out Cesar, who was laboring in apricot orchards near San Jose. Ross became his mentor, teacher and best friend. Together, they would propel the plight of migrant farm workers into the national spotlight.■

Cesar Chavez co-founded the United Farm Workers Union with union activist Dolores Huerta. Huerta, the mother of eleven, shared Chavez's belief in change through non-violence and traveled with Cesar throughout California encouraging workers to unionize.

LA CAUSA

CHAPTER
5

Ross hired Cesar to help him empower the Latino community. Cesar made 35 dollars a week. He was 25 years old and it was the most money he'd ever made. Cesar worked with Ross to organize CSO chapters across California. Under Cesar's guidance, CSO became the most militant and effective Latino civil rights group of its day, assisting Latinos to become citizens, registering them to vote, challenging police brutality and pressuring local governments to improve barrio conditions. Cesar traveled throughout California and made speeches in support of workers' rights.

But Cesar's activism did little to make his life easier. He and Helen still struggled. To support their ever-growing family, she worked in the fields during the week and joined her husband on the weekends. Cesar often had to bring his youngest kids along when he traveled to various California farm communities because they couldn't afford a babysitter.

The message he gave was worth the hardships. He emphasized to his listeners that the only way to change their outrage at the conditions under which they lived was devoting their time to changing them. That would involve sacrifice. If they wanted to hold on to their current jobs and their way of life, they couldn't change anything.

He became general director of CSO in 1958 and received more money. But even so, Cesar's heart was still in the fields. His dream was to create an organization that protected the migrants. He repeatedly tried to convince CSO to turn their attention to organizing farm workers.

However, he eventually had to accept that he and CSO had come to a crossroad. So in 1962, Cesar followed his heart and resigned his paid position with CSO. He confessed later that he was terrified. It had been the first regular paying job he ever had. Cesar moved his wife and their eight children to Delano. There he founded the National Farm Workers Association, or NFWA.

Cesar was joined by another well-known activist, Dolores Huerta, who was a founding member of the Stockton chapter of the Community Service Organization. Pursuing social justice was literally in Dolores's blood. Her father, Juan Fernandez, had been a miner, field worker, union activist and state assemblyman. Her mother, Alicia Chavez, owned a restaurant and a 70-room hotel, which often put up farm worker families for free. Alicia encouraged her daughter to be outspoken and proactive. Dolores attended the University of Pacific's Delta Community College and earned a teaching degree. But her experiences in the classroom soon prompted her to leave teaching. Many of her students were the children of migrant workers, who came to class hungry and barefoot. She believed that she could be much more useful to them as an activist.

Armed with determination and fierce intelligence, Dolores lobbied for workers' rights. In 1961 she succeeded in having citizenship requirements removed from pension and public assistance programs. She helped push through legislation allowing people the right to vote and to take their driver's license test in Spanish. She was also instrumental in bringing an end to the *bracero* program.

Dolores and Cesar both believed it was vital to organize farm workers. So along with Cesar, Dolores resigned from the CSO. A single mom, Dolores also moved her seven children to Delano and there worked with Cesar to get their organization established. They agreed that the NFWA should have a symbol, so Cesar and his brother Richard created a flag. Richard drew an Aztec eagle and Cesar chose the black and red colors. The eagle was intentionally made as a simple design. That way, workers would be able to draw it on handmade red flags to wave as a show of unity. Cesar believed that symbols were very important. An Aztec eagle meant pride and dignity.

Cesar and Dolores spent the next couple of years traveling throughout California's San Joaquin Valley recruiting farm workers and their families. Cesar would later explain in his interview with Wendy Goepel how important it was to secure a solid foundation.

"The biggest problem of all is to build a group spirit and to keep people involved and concerned over a long period of time," he said. "You have to just begin this by finding the committed people in every little community; this takes time. A union, then, is not simply getting enough workers to stage a strike. A union is building a group with a spirit and an existence all its own."

The guiding principles behind the organization were based on human respect and the philosophies of nonviolence of Gandhi and Dr. Martin Luther King Jr. But Cesar was quick to point out that people shouldn't mistake nonviolence for passivity. He noted in a 1970 *Observer* interview that many people didn't truly understand what being nonviolent meant.

"People think nonviolence is really weak and non-militant," he said. "Nonviolence takes more guts, if I can put it bluntly, than violence. Most violent acts are accomplished by getting the opponent off guard, and it doesn't take that much character. Nonviolence is most powerful in the action situation where people are using nonviolence because they want desperately to bring about some change. Nonviolence in action is a very potent force and it can't be stopped. No man-made law, no human ruler, no army can destroy this. There is no way it can be destroyed, except by those within the nonviolent struggle. And so, if we have the capacity to endure, if we have the patience, things will change."

As always, Cesar referred back to Gandhi. He told the *Observer* that "Gandhi showed how a whole nation could be liberated without an army. He showed us not by talking, not by what he wrote as much as by his actions, his own willingness to live by truth and by respect for mankind and accepting the sacrifices. You see, nonviolence exacts a very high price from one who practices it. But once you are able to meet that demand then you can do most things, provided you have the time."

It was the right time for the right movement. Even after the *bracero* program ended in 1964, Mexican migrant workers continued to be hired for low-paying farm work. But the days of employers being able to intimidate unions out of existence were about to come to an end. By the mid-1960s, America was in the grip of a cultural revolution that was redefining who we were as a country. Minorities were encouraged to make their presence felt. A wave of Chicano activism, especially on college campuses, made it a favorable environment for Latino labor organizing.

In September 1965, Filipino members of the Agricultural Workers Organizing Committee (AWOC) went on strike against Delano area grape growers, demanding higher wages. At first, the situation caught Dolores and Cesar off guard. They had planned to spend several more years recruiting members for their organization before engaging in a confrontation as risky as a strike. But they quickly realized that they had to support their fellow workers. On September 16, 1965, the NFWA voted to join in what became famous as the Delano Grape Strike. The two groups decided to concentrate their efforts on a single grower, the Schenley Corporation. Over 5,000 grape workers walked off their jobs in what would be a long, bitter dispute.

In March 1966, Cesar organized a march of more than 300 miles from Delano to the state capital of Sacramento. He was at the head of a group of farm workers and supporters who carried banners that proclaimed *Viva La Causa!* which meant "long live our cause!" They began with less than 100 marchers. They reached Sacramento with more than 10,000. They wanted the state government to pass laws which would permit farm workers to organize into a union and allow collective bargaining agreements. Shortly after the march, the Schenley Corporation signed the first-ever farm labor agreement.

That same year, AWOC and NFWA merged to form the United Farm Workers Organizing Committee, or UFWOC.

But Cesar knew staging a strike wasn't enough. Public awareness had to be raised and public support garnered. So he and Dolores encouraged all Americans to boycott table grapes as a show of support. Cesar also built a broad coalition among religious, student and community organizations. And in 1968, Cesar went through a public 25-day fast—a period in which he didn't eat anything—to further draw attention to the cause of migrant workers.

In the end, the strike lasted five years. By 1970, the effects of the boycott convinced most table grape growers to sign contracts with the UFWOC and its members. But Cesar knew it was simply a small victory in what would be a long, ongoing struggle.■

Chavez's national boycott of table grapes in California led to the passage of the Agricultural Labor Relations Act. Still the only law of its kind in the nation, it guarantees California farm workers the right for unions to bargain for better wages and working conditions and is one of Chavez's greatest legacies.

AN ACTIVIST TO THE END

Although the UFWOC had won a significant battle, the war was far from over. Soon after the grape growers signed their contracts, vegetable growers in the Salinas Valley signed contracts called "sweetheart deals" with the Teamsters Union. This was the growers' way of preventing the UFWOC from unionizing their workers. They knew that the Teamsters wouldn't pressure them in the way that Cesar would.

He reacted by calling for a lettuce boycott. The growers went to court to try to force him to end the boycott. The court sided with the growers. Because Cesar refused to stop the boycott, he was put in jail in December 1970.

Citizens, both private and public, were outraged. Once again, the struggle being waged in the fields of California became national news. Those close to Cesar frequently worried about his safety. More than one striker had been killed during the labor unrest as passions ran high among growers.

Hoping to prevent a similar situation in their state, the Arizona legislature passed a law banning the right of farm workers to strike or boycott in 1971. Cesar responded by fasting for 25 days in Phoenix, gaining the support and sympathy of people all across the country. It seemed that with each effort to break the union and keep the workers under their thumbs, the growers succeeded in actually promoting the union's cause. Their actions brought the workers' injustices into clearer focus for the average citizen.

In 1972, Cesar led the UFWOC into the AFL-CIO, the national organization of labor unions in the U.S., as an official member. Its name became the United Farm Workers of America, or UFW. He also moved the union's headquarters from Delano to a new site 50 miles south. Located on the slope of the Tehachapi Mountains that separate the San Joaquin Valley from Los Angeles, it was called La Paz ("The Peace").

When the table grape agreements came up for renegotiation in 1973, the growers instead signed with the Teamsters, prompting 10,000 farm workers to walk off their jobs in protest. Cesar immediately called for a new worldwide grape boycott. By 1975 polls indicated that 17 million Americans were honoring it. The public's support of the grape workers' cause forced growers to accept California's then-Governor Jerry Brown's collective bargaining law for farm workers. Called the Agricultural Labor Relations Act of 1976, the groundbreaking legislation remains the *only* law in the nation that protects the farm workers' right to unionize.

For the rest of the decade, Cesar would continue using the power of nonviolence to win contracts for UFW workers. By the early 1980s, almost 80,000 farm workers were working under UFW contracts that gave them higher pay, family health coverage, pension benefits and other protections. But the growers weren't ready to accept defeat.

In 1982, George Deukmejian was elected governor of California. The growers contributed more than one million dollars to his campaign. After taking office, Deukmejian shut down enforcement of the state's historic farm labor law. Thousands of farm workers lost their UFW contracts. Workers were fired and blacklisted. Some were even killed. The situation threatened to spiral out of control so Cesar announced a third grape boycott in 1984.

Four years later, at the age of 61, he endured a grueling 36-day "Fast for Life" as part of an ongoing campaign to protest the reversal of the farm workers' hard-earned rights, the denial of free elections and to promote public awareness of pesticide poisoning of grape workers and their children.

Asked why he would subject himself again to the suffering of a fast, Cesar explained the power behind fasting on the UFW website.

"A fast is first and foremost personal," he said. "It is a fast for the purification of my own body, mind, and soul. The fast is also a heartfelt prayer for purification and strengthening for all those who work beside me in the farm worker movement. The fast is also an act of penance for those in positions of moral authority and for all men and women activists who know what is right and just, who know that they could and should do more. The fast is finally a declaration of non-cooperation with supermarkets who promote and sell and profit from California table grapes."

He was also becoming increasingly aware of the ravaging effects that pesticides—especially those that were sprayed on table grapes—were having on migrant workers. By extension, everyone who ate food raised using pesticides was in danger. He chose the celebration of Dr. Martin Luther King Day in 1990 to give a speech expressing his concerns.

"The evil is far greater than even I had thought it to be," he told his listeners. "It threatens to choke out the life of our people and also the life system that supports us all. The prestigious National Academy of Sciences recently concluded an exhaustive five-year study which determined that pesticides do not improve profits and do not produce more crops."

The speech continued as Cesar described how children living in communities surrounded by the grape fields were in almost constant contact with pesticides: "when they play outside, when they drink the water, and when they hug their parents returning from the fields. And the children are dying. They are dying slow, painful, cruel deaths in towns called cancer clusters, in cancer clusters like McFarland, where the children cancer rate is 800 percent above normal. These same pesticides can be found on the grapes you buy in the stores.

"The solution to this deadly crisis will not be found in the arrogance of the powerful, but in solidarity with the weak and helpless. I pray to God that this fast will be a preparation for a multitude of simple deeds for justice. Carried out by men and women whose hearts are focused on the suffering of the poor and who yearn, with us, for a better world. Together, all things are possible."

Though the fast clearly weakened his system, Cesar refused to stop his actions on behalf of farm workers. In 1993 he traveled to Arizona to help defend the union against a lawsuit brought on by a powerful grower.

Cesar Chavez died in his sleep on April 23, 1993, in San Luis, Arizona. It was just a few miles from where he had been born. His brother Richard built a simple wooden casket and Cesar's body was placed inside. Then it was transported to Delano, where a procession of 50,000 people marched alongside in his honor. Mourners came from all over the United States for what was the largest-ever funeral of any American labor leader. He was buried at the union's headquarters in La Paz, in a rose garden at the foot of a hill he often climbed to watch the sunrise.

According to the UFW website: "Cesar gave his last ounce of strength defending the farm workers in this case," stated his successor, UFW President Arturo Rodriguez, who was with him in Arizona during the trial. "He died standing up for their First Amendment right to speak out for themselves."

Cesar left behind a rich legacy, embodied in his life-long motto: *sí se puede* ("It can be done"). In 1994 he was posthumously awarded the Presidential Medal of Freedom, the highest civilian honor in America.

Cesar Chavez's optimism, compassion and dedication affected people from all walks of life. To everyone from politicians and Hollywood celebrities to migrant workers, he was a true hero. The late Senator Robert F. Kennedy called Cesar "one of the heroic figures of our time."

But his notoriety and fame never changed who Cesar was. Many companies and organizations offered him high-paying consulting jobs but he turned them all down. He didn't want to lose touch with the people he had dedicated his life to helping.

Amazingly, Cesar never earned more than $6,000 a year. What he lacked in material possessions was more than made up for by the love and respect of millions.■

CHRONOLOGY

1927   Born on March 31 in Yuma, Arizona

1938   Chavez family loses their farm in Great Depression and become migrant farm workers

1942   Quits school to work in the fields after his father is hurt in a car accident

1944   Enlists in the Navy and sees active duty in the Pacific

1946   Joins the National Agricultural Workers Union

1948   Marries Helen Fabela

1952   Begins working with the Community Service Organization

1962   Forms the National Farm Workers Association (NFWA)

1965   Filipino grape pickers go on strike to improve wages and Cesar's NFWA joins in the strike a week later

1966   Merges NFWA with the Agricultural Workers Organizing
        Committee (AWOC) to form United Farm Workers Organizing
        Committee (UFWOC)

1968   Undergoes 25-day fast to promote support for union organizing
        efforts and nonviolence; in March, announces plans for a Cali-
        fornia grape boycott

1970   Goes to jail for refusing to obey court order against boycotting
        lettuce growers

1971   Fasts for 24 days to protest Arizona law banning farm workers'
        right to strike or boycott

1972   Leads UFWOC into AFL-CIO, where it changes name to
        United Farm Workers of America (UFW); moves headquarters
        to La Paz.

1973   Begins second grape boycott after growers won't renew con-
        tracts

1984   Begins third grape boycott

1988   Has 36-day public fast, his longest-ever, to call attention to farm
        workers and their children made ill by pesticide usage

1990   Signs agreement in April with the Mexican government that
        allows Mexican farm workers to provide medical benefits to
        families still in Mexico

1991   Is awarded Mexico's highest civilian honor, the Aguila Azteca

1993   Dies in San Luis, Arizona on April 23

1994   Is posthumously awarded the U.S. Medal of Freedom by Presi-
        dent Bill Clinton in April; California governor Pete Wilson
        designates March 21 as Cesar Chavez day, a state holiday

2003   Is honored by release of U.S. Postal Service stamp bearing his
        likeness on 10th anniversary of his death

TIMELINE IN HISTORY

1910 The Mexican Revolution causes many Mexicans to come to the U.S. Southwest looking for work, where they become a source of cheap farm labor.

1918 Mexicans are actively recruited to work in the American Southwest.

1924 Immigration Act allows unlimited admission of Mexican workers.

1928 Corky Gonzales, future Community Organizer for Mexican Americans, is born; Confederacion de Uniones Obreras Mexicanas (CUOM) is formed to organize Mexican workers in the U.S.

1929 Stock Market crashes on October 29, marking the beginning of the Great Depression.

1931 Rose Pesotta unionizes female Mexican-American garment workers in Los Angeles.

1936 Bert Corona organizes unions for cannery and warehouse workers.

1938 On assignment for *The Light* newspaper, singer/social activist Woody Guthrie investigates conditions of migrant workers.

1939 John Steinbeck's *The Grapes of Wrath* is published, which illustrates the poverty of migrant workers in the California grape-growing industry.

1942 *Bracero* program begins, allowing Mexican nationals to work in the Southwest as a source of cheap labor.

1951 Public Law 78 passes, allowing U.S. farmers to hire *braceros* if there is a shortage of local labor.

1952   The Agricultural Workers Organizing Committee (AWOC) is founded in Stockton, California by Father Donald McDonnell, Father Thomas McCullough and Dolores Huerta.

1964   The *bracero* program ends.

1968   Senator Robert F. Kennedy and Dr. Martin Luther King are assassinated.

1970   Contract agreements are reached between the UFW and most major grape growers.

1972   California voters soundly defeat Proposition 22, which would have outlawed boycotting and limited secret ballot elections to full-time farm workers.

1975   California Supreme Court outlaws the use of the *cortito*, a short handled hoe.

1976   California becomes first major agricultural state to grant farm workers the right to unionize.

1986   On November 6, Congress approves the Immigration Reform and Control Act making it illegal for employers to hire undocumented workers.

FOR FURTHER READING

For Young Adults:

Altman, Linda Jacobs. *The Importance of Cesar Chavez*. San Diego, CA: Lucent Books, 1996.

Atkin, S. Beth. *Voices from the Fields: Children of Migrant Farmworkers Tell Their Stories*. New York: Little Brown & Co., 2000.

Collins, David. *Farmworker's Friend: The Story of Cesar Chavez*. Minneapolis, MN: Carolrhoda Books, 1996.

Conord, Bruce W. *Cesar Chavez: Union Leader*. Broomall, PA: Chelsea House Publishers, 1992.

De Ruiz, Dana Catharine and Rudy Gutierrez (illustrator) and Richard Larios (contributor). *La Causa: The Migrant Farmworkers' Story (Stories of America)*. Austin, TX: Raintree/Steck-Vaughn, 1996.

Krull, Kathleen and Yuyi Morales (illustrator). *Harvesting Hope*. New York: Harcourt Children's Books, 2003.

Thatcher-Murcia, Rebecca. *Dolores Huerta*. Bear, DE: Mitchell Lane Publishers, 2003.

Zannos, Susan. *Cesar Chavez*. Bear, DE: Mitchell Lane Publishers, 1999.

Works Consulted:

California Curriculum Project. "Cesar E. Chavez's Biography." Hispanic Biographies, 1994. http://www.sfsu.edu/~cecipp/cesar_chavez/cesarbio5-12.htm

(continued on next page)

Chavez, Cesar. "Lessons of Dr. Martin Luther King, Jr." Speech given on January 12, 1990. http://www.sfsu.edu/~cecipp/cesar_chavez/cesarmlk.htm

Ferriss, Susan and Ricardo Sandoval. *The Fight in the Fields: Cesar Chavez and the Farmworkers Movement.* New York: Harcourt Brace & Company, 1997.

Goepel, Wendy. "Viva la Causa." Interview with Cesar Chavez. Farm Labor, April 1964. http://www.sfsu.edu/~cecipp/cesar_chavez/lacausa.htm

Matthiessen, Peter and Ilan Stavans. *Sal Si Puedes (Escape If You Can): Cesar Chavez and the New American Revolution.* Berkeley, CA: University of California Press, 2000.

Nelson, Eugene. *Huelga! The First Hundred Days of the Great Delano Grape Strike.* Delano, CA: Farm Worker Press, 1966.

ON THE WEB

Cesar E. Chavez Institute for Public Policy
http://www.sfsu.edu/~cecipp/cesar_chavez/chavezhome.htm

Official Web Page of the United Farm Workers
http://www.ufw.org

Si Se Puede! Cesar E. Chavez and His Legacy
http://clnet.ucr.edu/research/chavez/

GLOSSARY

adobe (ah-DOE-bee) - type of brick made of clay, straw and water

barrio - urban neighborhood predominantly populated by Mexican Americans and largely Spanish-speaking people

boycott - an organized protest in which people are asked not to buy certain products as a way to apply pressure on an employer to unionize

bracero (brah-SAIR-oh) - Mexican day laborer working in the US on contract.

Chicano (chi-CAW-no) - American of Mexican descent

cortito (core-TEE-to)- a short handled hoe

drought (drowt)- period of abnormally dry weather

epiphany (ee-PIFF-an-ee) - sudden flash of inspiration that reveals something important

erode (ee-ROAD) - wear away over a period of time

livestock - animals such as cattle, chickens or goats raised in large number

papal encyclical (PAY-pull en-SICK-li-cal) - letter from the Roman Catholic Pope with his views on a particular subject

peon (PEE-ahn) - farmworker or unskilled laborer, often bound to their employer by harsh credit terms

recession - significant decline in economic activity, which generally results in higher prices and unemployment.

scabs - workers who cross a picket line and take the place of striking workers

transient (TRAN-see-ent) - person passing through an area with only brief stops

union (YOON-yun) - organization of workers overseeing wages, benefits, and working conditions

yellow-dog contracts - written contracts signed by employees promising not to join a union while they are employed

INDEX